THE GOSPEL OF JOHN

WHO IS JESUS?

LEVEL 2

AUTHORS J. WESLEY EBY
AND PAULA TROUTMAN

BEACON HILL PRESS
OF KANSAS CITY

CONTENTS

Pronunciation Guide

Vowels

Symbol	Key Words	Usual Letters
ay	age, day	a, ai, ay
a	ask, cat	a
ah	father, ox	a, o
aw	auto, saw	a, au, aw
ee	each, see	e, ee, ea, ey, y
e	egg, bed	e
air	pair, bear	air, are, ear
er	her, bird	er, ir, ur
ie	ice, pie	i, ie, y
i	inch, sit	i
oh	oat, no	o, oa, oe, ow
ew	new, moon	u, ew, oo, ue
oo	good, bush	oo, u
ou	out, cow	ou, ow
oy	oil, boy	oi, oy
yew	use, human	u
u*	up, just (final or only sound of a syllable)	u
uh*	mother, ago (First or middle sound of a word or syllable)	any vowel

Consonants

Symbol	Key Words	Usual Letters
b	boat, cab	b, bb
ch	church, match	ch, tch
d	day, dad	d, dd
f	foot, wife	f, ff, ph, gh
g	gate, big	g, gg
h	hand, behind	h, wh
j	joy, page	j, g, dg
k	king, music	k, c, ck, ch
ks	box, sacks	x, cks
kw	queen, equal	qu
l	life, hill	l, ll
m	man, ham	m, mm
n	new, son	n, nn, kn
ng	drink, sing	n, ng
p	pig, cap	p, pp
r	race, year	r, rr, wr
s	sun, face	s, c, ss, sc
sh	sheep, fish	sh, ti
t	teach, mat	t, tt
th	thin, bath	th
th	this, bathe	th
v	vine, love	v
w	win, away	w
y	you, beyond	y
z	zeal, bees	z, zz, s
zh	measure	s, z

*This is the same as the schwa sound found in many dictionaries.

INTRODUCTION

You, the learner, will study the Bible in this book. The Bible contains the words of God to us. We call it God's Word.

These lessons will help you learn about the Christian faith. You will study some of the teachings of Jesus Christ. You will learn some of the important things that Jesus taught. These lessons can help you become a Christian. If you are a Christian, these lessons can help you become a better Christian.

These lessons are for people who are learning English. They are also for people who are just learning to read English. These lessons will help people who are beginning to learn about the Bible. The writers want you to understand the Bible. They want you to understand the lessons. So, the sentences are not very long. Most of the words are words that you know. Or, the words will be easy for you to learn.

Your teacher will help you learn. Your teacher wants you to know about God and the Bible. So, do not be afraid to ask for help. Ask about the things you do not know or understand.

God loves you very much. He wants to be your God. He wants you to learn about Him. He wants you to believe in Jesus Christ. He wants Jesus to be your Savior.

You can pray and ask God to help you learn. He will help you know about Him. God will help you to believe His Word. Then, you will know God in your mind and in your heart.

—*Editor*

1 JESUS IS THE SON OF GOD

Memory Verse: ". . . Jesus is the Christ, the Son of God . . ." (John 20:31)

Scripture Lesson: John 1:1-5, 9-14; 20:30-31

In this book, we will answer the question, "Who is Jesus?" In this first lesson, we will learn that Jesus is the Son of God. In each lesson, we will learn something new about Jesus. We will enjoy learning the answer to the question, "Who is Jesus?"

John was a **disciple** of Jesus. He wrote the book called the "Gospel of John" in the Bible. John's book is about Jesus. Jesus said and did many wonderful things. John wrote about certain things that Jesus said and did. These things help us to know who Jesus is. John wanted us to understand who Jesus is. That is why John wrote the book.

A. JESUS, THE SON OF GOD, GIVES LIFE. (John 20:30-31)

John wanted our faith to grow. Faith is our belief and trust in God. We believe by faith that Jesus is the Son of God. Our faith should grow. It should be alive. Our faith is dead when we do not believe.

Jesus did many **amazing** acts. We call these acts **miracles.** John told us about some of them. The miracles showed the power of Jesus. John wrote about Jesus' miracles so we would believe in Jesus.

Today, the miracles help us understand that Jesus is the Son of God. They help us believe in Jesus. They help us have faith in Jesus. Then, we receive **eternal life** when we have faith in Jesus.

Our eternal life starts here on earth. It starts when we believe in Jesus. But, it continues even after our bodies die. Our spirits live forever in heaven. We will live with Jesus forever and ever.

B. GOD **CREATED** THE WORLD THROUGH JESUS, THE WORD. (John 1:1-5)

John called Jesus "the Word." John said, "In the beginning was the Word . . ." (verse 1) This means that Jesus has always lived. Jesus did not have a beginning. And, He will not have an end. Jesus was with God from the beginning.

Jesus came to earth as a man. He was born to Mary. Yet, He was the Son of God. He was the God-Man. Later, Jesus was killed on a cross. He died as a man dies. Then, He was raised to life again by God. Jesus was more than a man. He was God in a human body.

Jesus is God. John said, ". . . the Word was God." (verse 1) God created all things through Jesus. (verse 3) God created life through Jesus. Jesus is Life.

God gives us eternal life through Jesus. We are safe in Him. We have hope in Jesus even when our lives are difficult. We have this hope because there is life in Jesus. John said, "In Him [Jesus] was life . . ." (verse 4)

Jesus is the Light that God shines on us. (verse 5) Jesus came to be a Light to people. But, many people did not understand who Jesus was. They **opposed** Him and the things He did. There was great **darkness** in the world. Jesus came to be a Light in the darkness.

Jesus, the Light, shines in the darkness. The Light helps us to know God. The Light helps us to see our way to God. The Light helps us to see and know who Jesus is.

C. JESUS, THE SON OF GOD, TEACHES US ABOUT GOD.
(John 1:9-14)

Jesus came to our world. He became a real man. John said, "The Word became flesh . . ." (verse 14) His life showed us who God is. His life showed us what God is like. His words teach us the truth about God. In Jesus, we see all God's power. In Jesus, we see how great God is.

Jesus made the world and He was in the world. Still, many people did not know Him. Still, many people **refused** to believe that He was God's Son. (verses 10-11)

All people who believe in Jesus become children of God. (verse 12) They are born of God. They are **born again.** They receive new life through Jesus, the Son of God.

CONCLUSION

Who is Jesus? Jesus is the Son of God.

The Gospel of John tells us some important things about the Son of God. (1) Jesus is our **Savior.** He gives us eternal life. (2) God created everything through Jesus, His Son. (3) Jesus shows us who God is and what God is like.

John wanted us to have faith in Jesus. John wanted our faith to grow. Our faith grows as we understand who Jesus is. We must believe by faith that Jesus is really the Son of God.

QUESTIONS: *Fill in the blanks.*

1. Jesus is the _____ _____ _____.
2. Faith is our _____.
3. We receive _____ _____ when we believe in Jesus.
4. God created the _____ through Jesus.
5. John called Jesus "_____ _____."
6. Jesus teaches us about _____.
7. All people who believe in Jesus become

   _____ _____ _____.

8. Name 3 things that the Gospel of John tells us.
    (1) _____
    (2) _____
    (3) _____

Here are some questions for you to think about and discuss:

1. What do you believe about Jesus?
2. Is Jesus your Savior? How do you know that Jesus is your Savior?
3. How do we know what God is like?
4. How strong is your faith? How can you help your faith to grow?

VOCABULARY:

1. **disciple** *(noun):* a person who believes in and follows Jesus
2. **amazing** *(adjective):* very surprising; not expected; hard to believe
3. **miracles** *(noun):* things only God can do; things that people can do only with the help of God
4. **eternal life** *(noun phrase):* life without end; living forever in heaven with God
5. **created** *(verb):* made from nothing
6. **opposed** *(verb):* be against; fought against

7. **darkness** *(noun):* no light; In this lesson, "darkness" means a world of sin and evil.
8. **refused** *(verb):* not willing to accept; would not do something
9. **born again** *(adjective phrase):* describes a person who is a Christian; The first birth is when a person is born to parents. The second birth or being "born again" is when a person becomes God's child.
10. **Savior** *(proper noun):* Jesus Christ; the One who saves people from sin and hell

2 | JESUS IS THE CHRIST

Memory Verse: ". . . I believe that You are the Christ, the Son of God
. . ." (John 11:27)
Scripture Lesson: John 1:19-34

John the Baptist was a cousin of Jesus. He was not the same John
who wrote the Gospel of John. He was not one of Jesus' 12 disciples.
This was a different man named John.

John was called "the Baptist" because he **baptized** people. John
preached that people must repent of their sins. He said that God
would forgive their sins. (See Matthew 3:2, 11.)

John told other people about Jesus. He told them that Jesus was
coming. He said that Jesus was the Christ. John was a **witness**. He
was a witness for Jesus, the Christ.

A. JOHN THE BAPTIST TOLD US WHO HE WAS. (John 1:19-23)

John knew who he was. He knew that he was not the Christ. He
knew that he was not a **prophet.** John told the Jews this fact. He
would not accept any of these names for himself.

John knew that the important person was Jesus. God had
promised the Jews that He would send the **Messiah** (muh-SIE-uh).
Jesus was the promised Messiah. Jesus was the Christ. John knew that
Jesus Christ was coming soon. (Today, we usually say Jesus Christ
instead of Jesus, the Christ.)

John knew that he was to be a witness for Jesus Christ. His job
was to tell other people that Jesus was coming. The prophets said
that God was sending the Messiah. John knew that he was only a
witness to the Christ who was coming.

B. JOHN UNDERSTOOD THE IMPORTANCE OF JESUS.
    (John 1:24-28)

John understood that Jesus Christ was more important than he
was. The **Pharisees** (FAIR-uh-seez) asked why he baptized people.
John tried to get the Pharisees to think about Jesus. John did not
want them to think about himself. He did not want them to think
about what He did. He wanted them to think about the One they
did not know. That One was Jesus.

John knew that Jesus was very important. John did not feel **worthy** to untie Jesus' sandals or shoes. John did not feel worthy to be a servant of Jesus. He knew that Jesus was greater than he was. John knew that Jesus was greater than all other men. Jesus is greater because He is the Christ. John told people that Jesus was greater.

We should be a witness like John was. We should not get attention for ourselves. The attention should be on Jesus. He is the One who is important. We must be careful as we witness. We do not **win people** to ourselves. We must win people to Jesus.

C. JOHN WAS A FAITHFUL WITNESS. (John 1:29-34)

Jesus **existed** before John. Jesus has always existed. Jesus was with God from the beginning. Jesus was with God before He came to earth. John said that is why Jesus is more important. John believed that Jesus is the Son of God. He believed that Jesus was the Christ that God promised. John's faith was great. His witness was great because his faith was great.

John called Jesus the "Lamb of God." (verse 29) Jesus came to take away the sins of all people. We cannot remove the sin that separates us from God. Only God can remove sin. God removes our sin through Jesus.

Jesus is our Savior. Jesus takes away our sin. Jesus brings us back to God. This was the good news John had to tell! This is also the good news we have to tell today!

Jesus will also give us the Holy Spirit. God gave Jesus the Holy Spirit. Jesus promised to give the Holy Spirit to us. The Holy Spirit is our Helper.

John did not use many words to tell about Jesus. But, he did not forget anything important. John told us how to witness. He also showed us how to witness.

Today, we must witness for Jesus. Jesus wants us to witness for Him. He said, ". . . you will be My witnesses . . ." (Acts 1:8) The Holy Spirit will help us to witness. We must witness wherever we are. We must witness to our family and friends. We must witness to our neighbors and people at work. We must be true witnesses of Jesus, the Christ.

CONCLUSION

Who is Jesus? Jesus is the Christ. And, John the Baptist was a true witness for Jesus Christ. John said that Jesus Christ was coming. He said that Jesus was the Messiah that God promised.

Today, we witness when we tell other people about Jesus Christ. He is our Savior. We witness because we are thankful. We are thankful that Jesus has saved us from all our sins. We are thankful that Jesus is the Christ, the promised Messiah.

QUESTIONS: *Fill in the blanks.*

1. John the Baptist said that Jesus was the _____.
2. Another name for the Christ is the _____.
   The _____ said that God was sending the Messiah.
3. Jesus is _____ than all other men.
4. John's witness was great because his _____ in Jesus was great.
5. Jesus is our _____. He takes away our _____.
6. Jesus gives us the _____ _____ to be our Helper.
7. Jesus said, ". . . you will be My _____ . . ."
8. We witness when we tell other people about _____ _____.

Here are some questions for you to think about and discuss:

1. Who was John the Baptist?
2. Why was Jesus Christ more important than John the Baptist?
3. How does the Holy Spirit help us today?
4. Are you a witness for Jesus? How can you be a better witness?

VOCABULARY:

1. **baptized** *(verb):* put people under water and bring them up again; an important way in which Christians show they are followers of Jesus
2. **witness** *(noun):* a person who tells what he has seen or knows; a person who tells what Jesus Christ has done for him

3. **prophet** *(noun):* a person who speaks for God; A prophet gives a message from God to people.
4. **Messiah** *(proper noun):* Jesus Christ; the Savior that God promised to send to earth
5. **Pharisees** *(proper noun):* religious leaders of the Jews
6. **worthy** *(adjective):* feel important enough
7. **win people** *(verb phrase):* make people believe in you; help people to believe in Jesus Christ
8. **existed** *(verb):* lived; was

3 | JESUS IS OUR KING

Memory Verse: ". . . He is Lord of lords and King of kings . . ."
   (Revelation 17:14)
Scripture Lesson: John 12:12-26

Jesus lived on earth for 33 years. He did many miracles. He made sick people well. He made blind people see. He healed **lame** people so they could walk. He even brought dead people back to life. Jesus was able to do miracles because He is God's Son.

Jesus wanted people to know that God loved them. He taught the people about the love of God. He taught His disciples and the people many things. And, many people believed in Jesus. They believed that He is the Son of God. These people accepted the love of God. They became **followers** of Jesus.

A.   JESUS WAS **HONORED** AS A KING. (John 12:12-19)

Many people were in the city of Jerusalem (juh-REW-suh-lum). They had come to the city for the **Passover** (PAS-OH-ver). Jesus was on His way to Jerusalem, too. He found a young donkey. (verse 14) He rode into the city on the donkey.

The people heard that Jesus was coming. Many of them knew about Jesus. Some of them had seen Jesus. The people knew about His miracles. They wanted to see Jesus. They wanted to honor Him.

Many people went to meet Jesus on the road. They waved **palm** branches. They shouted, "**Hosanna!**" They praised Jesus. They even called Jesus their King. (verse 13)

Each year, we remember this event in Jesus' life. We call this special day Palm Sunday. It is always the Sunday before Easter.

Jesus knew that He would die on a cross soon. He knew that His death would make Him a king. So, Jesus let the crowd call Him a king. Jesus did not stop the crowd from honoring Him.

Many things were written about Jesus before He came to earth. These things are called **prophecies**. Prophecies were messages God gave to His people. God gave these messages through prophets. Prophets spoke for God. They taught other people about God. They gave messages to the people from God.

14

God promised His people a Savior. The prophets told the people about this promise. Jesus is the Savior that God had promised.

The Bible has many prophecies about Jesus. Jesus **fulfilled** one prophecy when He rode on the donkey. (verse 15) Jesus fulfilled more prophecies in the days before His death. But, many people did not understand this. They did not know that Jesus was the promised Savior. They did not know that Jesus was fulfilling prophecies.

B. THE **GLORY** OF JESUS WAS IN HIS DEATH. (John 12:20-26)

Jesus knew that He was fulfilling prophecies. Jesus knew that His death would fulfill a prophecy. He knew that His death would be His glory.

Jesus' death would give life to people. Jesus explained this in verse 24. He said that a grain of wheat must fall to the ground and die. Then, it grows and becomes a wheat plant. It makes many seeds. These seeds make new plants. But, the grain cannot make more seeds if it does not die. The grain gives life to other plants by dying.

Jesus is like the grain of wheat. Because He died, people receive life. Jesus died to give life to us.

Jesus says we must be like Him. We must follow Him. We must give our lives to Jesus. We give our lives to Him by following Him. We do what He wants us to do. We tell other people about Him. We give our lives to Him. We let Him be our **Lord.**

The glory of Jesus was in His death. He received His glory when He gave His life for us. We receive our glory when we give our lives to Him. We give our lives by serving Jesus.

We must become servants of Jesus. God will honor those who serve Jesus. (verse 26) Our glory will be eternal life. We will live with Jesus forever.

CONCLUSION

Who is Jesus? He is our King. He is our Lord.

The people honored Jesus as He rode into Jerusalem. They called Him their king. They gave Him glory. But, the glory of Jesus was in His death. His glory was in giving His life. We are called to be like Jesus. We are called to give our lives. We must love Jesus. We must serve Him. We give Jesus glory by giving Him our lives. Jesus must be Lord of our lives. He must be our King.

QUESTIONS: *Give the answers.*

1. Where was Jesus going? _____

2. What did the people call Jesus? _____

3. Each year, we remember the event in Jesus' life from this lesson. What is this day called? _____

   _____

4. What do we call the messages that God gave to people through the prophets? _____

5. Why did Jesus die? _____

   _____

6. What must we give to Jesus? _____ _____

7. Whom must we love more than ourselves? _____

8. What do we receive when we give God our lives?

   _____ _____

Here are some questions for you to think about and discuss:

1. Why is Palm Sunday an important day for Christians?

2. How do prophecies about Jesus help us understand who He is?

3. Is Jesus your king? How can you honor Him as your king?

4. What does the memory verse mean, ". . . He is Lord of lords King of kings . . ."?

VOCABULARY:

1. **lame** *(adjective):* describes a person who cannot walk

2. **followers** *(noun):* people who follow someone else; Followers of Jesus are Christians; they believe in Jesus as their Savior.

3. **honored** *(verb):* respected; thought to be very important

4. **Passover** *(proper noun):* a special feast of the Jews each year; The Jews remembered how God helped them to leave Egypt and go to Israel.

5. **palm** *(noun):* a type of tree that grows in countries where the weather is warm all year

16

6. **Hosanna** *(interjection):* a word that means "save us;" It is used as a word of praise.

7. **prophecies** *(noun):* messages from God about things that will happen in the future

8. **fulfilled** *(verb):* made something come true; caused something to happen

9. **glory** *(noun):* being important and great; importance and greatness; also, praise and honor

10. **Lord** *(proper noun):* "lord" means a person who rules the lives of people; "Lord" is Jesus Christ, the One who rules our lives and we obey Him.

4 JESUS IS OUR LIVING LORD

Memory Verse: "... 'I have seen the Lord'! ..." (John 20:18)
Scripture Lesson: John 20:1-18

Jesus is the Christ, the Son of God. Jesus died for us. He gave His life so that we can have eternal life. We have eternal life by believing in Jesus. Because Jesus gave His life for us, we give our lives to Him. We give our lives by following and serving Him.

Jesus gave His life on the Cross. He was captured and **put on trial.** Then, Jesus was **crucified.** His followers put Him in a tomb. They did not understand why Jesus had to die. They were sad. Jesus was dead.

A. MARY AND THE DISCIPLES FOUND AN EMPTY TOMB. (John 20:1-9)

Mary Magdalene (MAG-duh-leen) was a follower of Jesus. Mary went to the tomb where Jesus was buried. She saw that the tomb was open. The stone was moved away from the door. Mary ran to Simon Peter and another disciple. (The other disciple probably was the John who wrote the Gospel of John.) She told them that Jesus was gone. She thought that robbers had taken the body of Jesus.

Peter and John ran to the tomb. The tomb was empty, just as Mary had told them. But, they found pieces of **linen** cloth in the tomb. They also found the **burial cloth.** The cloth was put on Jesus' body when He was buried. The disciples knew that robbers had not taken the body of Jesus. Robbers would not have removed the cloth from Jesus' body. The disciples believed that Jesus was alive. Yet, they still did not understand.

B. MARY SAW THE ANGELS AND THE **GARDENER.** (John 20:10-15)

The two disciples went home. But Mary stayed at the tomb. She was crying as she sat by the tomb. She did not believe that Jesus was alive. She believed that someone had taken His body.

Mary looked inside the tomb. She saw two angels. They were sitting where the body of Jesus had been. The angels asked Mary why she was crying. Mary told them that the body of Jesus was gone. She thought His body was stolen.

Mary did not wait for an answer from the angels. She turned away from the tomb. She was still crying. Then, Mary saw Jesus. She did not **recognize** Him. She thought He was the gardener. Jesus asked Mary why she was crying. He asked her whom she was looking for. Mary still believed that Jesus was dead. She thought he had helped take Jesus away. Mary wanted to know where the body of Jesus was. She wanted to find Jesus.

C. MARY BELIEVED THAT JESUS WAS ALIVE. (John 20:16-18)

Jesus said Mary's name. Then, she recognized Him. She knew that He was Jesus. She believed that Jesus was alive.

Mary had a new faith. Faith is more than knowing about Jesus. Faith is more than knowing what Jesus said and did. Faith is knowing Jesus. It is having a **personal relationship** with Jesus. John wrote his book to make our faith greater. This is the type of faith John is talking about. This is the faith that Mary had.

Jesus told Mary not to hold on to Him. Jesus wanted Mary to believe in Him. He wanted her faith to be greater. Jesus would not always be with Mary. Jesus was going to His Father in heaven. But, His Spirit would always be with her.

Today, we do not have Jesus in His body. But, we do have His Spirit. The Holy Spirit is our Helper. Jesus sent the Holy Spirit to be with us. Jesus sent the Spirit because He could not be with us in His body.

Jesus told Mary to go to the disciples. Mary told the disciples the good news. Mary said, "I have seen the Lord!" (verse 18) She told them that Jesus was alive. She shared her faith with the disciples.

CONCLUSION

Who is Jesus? He is our living Lord.

Mary Magdalene had new faith. She believed that Jesus was alive again. She knew Jesus in a personal relationship. Mary believed the Spirit of Jesus would always be with her. She shared her new faith with the disciples.

We must share our faith with other Christians, also. They need to know that they are not alone. They need to know that there are other people who believe in Jesus.

Christians should be happy with the good news. Jesus is alive! He is our living Lord!

QUESTIONS: *Give the answers.*

1. Who is the Son of God? _____
2. How did Jesus give His life for us? _____
   _____
3. Who went to the tomb and found it empty? _____
   _____
4. What did Mary believe when she saw the empty tomb?
   _____
5. When did Mary know Jesus was alive? _____
   _____
6. What words mean "knowing Jesus as your Savior"?
   _____   _____
7. Who is our Helper today? _____   _____
8. What is the good news that believers should be happy with?
   _____

Here are some questions for you to think about and discuss:

1. Do you believe that Jesus is alive? How do you know Jesus is alive?
2. How can you have a personal relationship with Jesus?
3. How can you share your faith with other people?
4. Why should you be happy with the good news that "Jesus is alive?"

VOCABULARY:

1. **put on trial** *(verb phrase):* question someone in a court of law to decide if the person is guilty
2. **crucified** *(verb):* killed by hanging on a cross; Jesus was nailed to the Cross.
3. **linen** *(noun):* a type of cloth
4. **burial cloth** *(noun phrase):* a cloth wrapped around people when they are buried
5. **gardener** *(noun):* a person who takes care of a garden

6. **recognize** *(verb):* know someone by looking at them
7. **personal relationship** *(noun phrase):* knowing Jesus as your Savior; knowing you are saved from your sins; knowing that you belong to God and you are His child

5 JESUS IS THE WAY TO GOD

Memory Verse: ". . . I [Jesus] am the Way and the Truth and the Life.
   . . ." (John 14:6)
Scripture Lesson: John 3:10-21; 5:19-20
Background Lesson: John 3:1-9; Numbers 21:4-9

Nicodemus (NIK-uh-DEE-mus) was an important man. He was a
ruler of the Jews. He was a Pharisee (FAIR-uh-see). He believed in
God.

One night, Nicodemus went to see Jesus. Nicodemus believed
that Jesus came from God. He wanted to talk to Jesus. And, Jesus
taught him many things.

A. JESUS GIVES ETERNAL LIFE. (John 3:10-15)

Nicodemus did not understand all the things Jesus said. He did
not understand about being born again. He asked Jesus some
questions. So, Jesus reminded him of a story from the Scripture. You
can read this story in Numbers 21:4-9.

The story is about the people of Israel (IZ-ree-ul) and their leader,
Moses. The **Israelites** (IZ-ree-uh-liets) were on their way from Egypt
(EE-jipt) to their land of Israel. They were in the desert. They were
not happy. They complained a lot.

God was not pleased that the Israelites complained. So, He sent
poisonous snakes among the people. The snakes bit the people, and
many of them died. The people begged Moses to help them. So,
Moses prayed to God.

God heard Moses' prayer and told him what to do. Moses made
a snake of **bronze.** He put the snake on a pole. The snake was lifted
up high in the air. Any person who was bitten by a poisonous snake
could look up. He looked up at the bronze snake and believed. Then,
the person lived. He did not die.

Jesus told Nicodemus that the people were just like the Israelites.
The people were dying in their sin. Yet, they could receive life. They
could receive eternal life if they look to Him, the **Son of Man.**

Jesus was lifted up on the Cross. He gives life to all people who
look to Him. He gives eternal life to all people who believe in Him.

22

B. JESUS IS THE ONLY WAY TO GOD. (John 3:16-21)

God loves the world. He loves all that He has created. God created people and He loves us. But, man sinned. Man **disobeyed** God. All people sin against God. God does not like our sin, yet He loves us very much.

So, God sent His Son, Jesus, to earth. God allowed His Son to die on the Cross. Jesus was the blood **sacrifice** for our sin. Jesus paid for our sins with His own blood. Jesus died to give us eternal life. Eternal life is for everyone. Eternal life is for anyone who believes in Jesus.

God does not want us to die in our sin. Our bodies will die, but our spirits will live forever. If we believe in Jesus, our spirits will live in heaven with God. This is eternal life. If we do not believe in Jesus, our spirits will **perish.** This is eternal death. We will be separated from God forever.

God sent Jesus to the world so that the world would not perish. We are the world. God sent Jesus to us. God sent Jesus because He loves us.

We must believe that Jesus is the Son of God. Jesus is the Way to God. Jesus is the only Way to eternal life.

We must also believe that we meet God through Jesus. We must believe that God forgives our sins. He forgives our sins when we **repent** of our sins. We must stop sinning. Then, we must believe that Jesus saves us from sin and hell. We must receive Jesus into our hearts and lives.

C. GOD SPEAKS AND WORKS THROUGH JESUS. (John 5:19-20)

Many people did not understand who Jesus was. They did not believe Jesus was the Son of God. He tried to tell the people who He was. He told them that God was His Father. Jesus said, ". . . I am from Him [God] and He sent Me." (John 7:29)

Jesus also said, "I and the Father are One." (John 10:30) Thus, Jesus' words are the words of God. Jesus' work is the work of God. God speaks through Jesus. And God works through Jesus. We know God because we know Jesus. Jesus is the only Way to God.

CONCLUSION

Who is Jesus? He is the Way. He is the Truth. He is the Life. Jesus came to earth to show us the Way to God. The Bible says, "For God so loved the world that He gave His one and only Son, that whoever believes in Him shall not perish but have eternal life." (John 3: 16)

QUESTIONS: *Fill in the blanks.*

1. Jesus gives_____ _____
   to all people who look to Him.
2. _____ sent His Son, Jesus, to earth to die for us.
3. Eternal life is for _____ who believes in
   Jesus.
4. Jesus died on the Cross for our _____.
5. Jesus is the only _____ to God.
6. God _____ our sins when we _____
   of our sins.
7. _____ and _____ are One.
8. Jesus said, "I am the _____ and the Truth and the
   _____."

Here are some questions for you to think about and discuss:

1. How did God show His love for all people?
2. "God loves you." How do you feel when you read that?
3. How can people know God? How do **YOU** know God?
4. What must you do to have eternal life?

VOCABULARY:

1. **Israelites** *(proper noun):* the people of the nation of Israel; the Jews
2. **poisonous** *(adjective):* describes something that can kill, destroy, or harm
3. **bronze** *(noun):* a type of metal that is yellow and brown
4. **Son of Man** *(proper noun phrase):* Jesus Christ; Jesus often called Himself the Son of Man.
5. **disobeyed** *(verb):* not obeyed; did not do what God said; did not obey the laws of God
6. **sacrifice** *(noun):* a gift given to God; God demanded a blood sacrifice for sin. Jesus died on the Cross and shed His blood as the sacrifice for all sin.

7. **perish** *(noun):* die; eternal death; being separated from God forever
8. **repent** *(verb):* are sorry for our sins; turn from our sins to God; ask God to forgive our sins

6 JESUS IS THE SOURCE OF LIVING WATER

Memory Verse: ". . . whoever drinks the water I [Jesus] give him will never thirst. . . ." (John 4:14)
Scripture Lesson: John 4:7-15, 25-29
Background Lesson: John 4:1-6

The Jews and Samaritans (suh-MAIR-uh-tunz) were two groups of people. They did not live in the same country. The Jews lived in Israel. The Samaritans lived in Samaria (suh-MAIR-ee-uh).

The Jews thought they were better than the Samaritans. So, the two groups did not like each other. They would not talk to each other.

Jesus was a Jew. One day, He met a woman from Samaria. In this lesson, we will learn what happened.

A. JESUS SHOWED US HOW TO LOVE. (John 4:7-13)

Jesus and His disciples were on a trip. On their way, they went through Samaria. It was noon, so they stopped to rest. There was a town nearby. Jesus sent His disciples to buy some food.

Jesus was sitting by a well. A Samaritan woman came to the well for water. Jesus asked her for some water to drink. The woman was surprised. She was a Samaritan, and Jesus was a Jew. Jews did not talk with Samaritans.

Jesus loved the woman. He did not care that she was a Samaritan. He wanted to help her. He had something to give her.

Today, we should love everyone. We should not care what country they are from. We should not look at the color of their skin. We should love all people. We must love them with God's love. We must share His love with everyone. We should love other people because God loves us.

B. JESUS OFFERED **LIVING WATER**. (John 4:14-15)

Jesus offered living water to the Samaritan woman. (verse 10) She did not understand what Jesus meant. She knew that the well was deep. Jesus did not have a bucket. He could not get the water out of the well. How could He give her a drink?

Jesus was talking about living water. He did not mean water out of the well. He was talking about eternal life. He called eternal life, "living water."

Jesus told the woman she would never be thirsty again. She still did not understand. She still thought Jesus was talking about water from the well. She asked Him for a drink of water. She was tired of walking to the well for water. She did not want to be thirsty again. But, she was talking about water from a well. She did not understand what living water was.

Today, Jesus offers living water to us. Living water is much better than water from a well. Living water fills us. It **satisfies** us. Living water fills our thirst for God. We have new life in God. We have eternal life through Jesus Christ.

C. JESUS IS THE MESSIAH. (John 4:25-29)

Jesus continued talking to the Samaritan woman. He wanted her to understand about living water. He wanted her to know who He was.

Jesus told the woman that He was the Messiah. (verses 25-26) The people were waiting for a Messiah. God had promised the Messiah. The people believed the Messiah would come. He would teach the people about God. And, He would **restore** the people to God. He would show the way to God. Jesus was the promised Messiah.

The Samaritan woman believed that a Messiah was coming. Jesus told her that He was that Messiah. And, she believed Him. She believed that Jesus was the Messiah. She ran back to town. She talked to all the people she knew. She told them that she had found the Messiah. She told them to come and see Jesus.

The woman from Samaria had received the living water. She believed that Jesus was the Messiah. He was her Savior. Jesus satisfied her thirst for God. Then, the living water flowed out of her. She told other people about Jesus. She told them about the living water.

Today, we can have the living water. We can be satisfied in our spirits. But, we must believe in Jesus. We must believe He is the Messiah. We must **admit** that we need the living water Jesus offers to us. Then, we will receive it. We will be satisfied.

CONCLUSION

Who is Jesus? Jesus is the **source** of living water. Living water does not come out of a well. It comes from God. Living water does not take away our **physical** thirst. But, it takes away our **spiritual** thirst.

Our spiritual thirst is satisfied. We have new life in Jesus Christ. Then, we want to tell other people. We want them to receive living water too.

QUESTIONS: *Give the answers.*

1. Who lived in Israel? the _____
   Who lived in Samaria? the _____
2. Why did Jesus surprise the Samaritan woman? _____
   _____
3. Why should we love other people? Because _____
   _____
4. What did Jesus offer the Samaritan woman?
   _____ _____
5. What is "living water?" _____
6. Whom did Jesus say He was? the _____
7. What did the woman do after she believed in Jesus?
   _____
8. What does the living water take away?
   _____

Here are some questions for you to think about and discuss:

1. How can you show love to all people? How can you love people who are different from you?
2. What do you believe living water is? How can you get living water today?
3. Are you thirsty for God? How can your thirst for God be satisfied?

VOCABULARY:

1. **living water** *(noun phrase):* new life in Jesus Christ; eternal life; words that Jesus used to describe the new life of a Christian
2. **satisfies** *(verb):* pleases; makes a person not thirsty or hungry
3. **restore** *(verb):* bring back; return
4. **admit** *(verb):* say that you know

5. **source** *(noun):* a place where something begins; a beginning point
6. **physical** *(adjective):* describes something of the body
7. **spiritual** *(adjective):* describes something of the spirit

7 JESUS IS THE BREAD OF LIFE

Memory Verse: "I [Jesus] am the Bread of Life." (John 6:48)
Scripture Lesson: John 6:34-51
Background Lesson: John 6:1-13, 22-31

One day, Jesus was speaking to a large crowd. It became late. The people were hungry. There was no food to give them. The disciples did not have money to buy food.

A young boy in the crowd had a lunch. He had five loaves of bread and two small fish. The boy gave his lunch to Jesus. Jesus thanked God for it. Then, Jesus broke the bread and fish into pieces.

Jesus told the disciples to give the food to the people. There were 5,000 men in the crowd. There was enough food for all of the people. There were even some baskets of food left over. This was a great miracle! Jesus used this miracle to teach the people.

A. JESUS UNDERSTANDS OUR HUNGER. (John 6:34)

The crowd was excited. Jesus had done a great miracle. He had fed a large crowd with a boy's lunch.

The next day, the crowd was still excited. They went looking for Jesus. They wanted to see another miracle.

Jesus saw the crowd. He knew they were hungry. But, Jesus knew they were not hungry for loaves of bread. They were not hungry for food we eat. The people were hungry in their spirits. They were hungry for the Bread of Life. Jesus wanted to satisfy their hunger. So, He talked to the people about the Bread of Life.

B. JESUS CAN SATISFY OUR HUNGER. (John 6:40-42)

Jesus told the people that He is the Bread of Life. Anyone who believes in Him receives life. This life is eternal life. Eternal life is living forever with Jesus in heaven.

Jesus told the people that He came down from heaven. But, the people did not understand this truth. They only knew Jesus as the son of Joseph and Mary. Some people became angry at Jesus' words.

The crowd had never heard these words before. They did not understand them. What did the words mean? "Jesus is the Son of God." "Jesus came down from heaven." "Believe in Jesus." Most of the people did not believe in Jesus. They did not believe Him even after seeing the miracle.

The people were **disappointed.** They wanted to see another miracle. They wanted more food to eat. They did not understand about the Bread of Life. They were not happy with the way Jesus was talking.

Today, people are still hungry in their spirits. We want to satisfy our hunger. But, we need more than bread for our bodies. We need the Bread of Life. That is why we believe in Jesus, the Son of God. He is the Bread of Life. He satisfies the hunger in our **souls.**

C. WE CAN HAVE THE BREAD OF LIFE. (John 6:35-39, 43-51)

We must believe to receive the Bread of Life. We must believe in Jesus. Believing is more than saying Jesus is the Son of God. Believing is more than saying that Jesus is a great teacher. Believing is **trusting** in Jesus. Believing is trusting what He taught. Believing is trusting in Jesus' death and **resurrection** to save us. Then, we receive eternal life.

We do not **deserve** eternal life. We cannot earn it. We cannot buy it. It is a gift from God. God offers us eternal life because He loves us. God gives us eternal life through Jesus, the Bread of Life.

Jesus, the Bread of Life, helps us grow as Christians. We grow by worshiping God. We grow by praying. We grow by reading the Bible. We grow by going to church. We grow as we obey what Jesus taught us. The Bread of Life helps us grow and become better Christians.

CONCLUSION

Who is Jesus? He is the Bread of Life.

People need to eat bread or food every day. Bread or food gives us strength for our bodies. This bread gives us physical life. But, the

Bread of Life gives us spiritual life. We receive new life in Jesus, the Bread of Life. And, He helps us grow in our lives as Christians.

We can have the Bread of Life. We can have eternal life even though we do not deserve it. God has made eternal life possible for every person. Let us thank God for the Bread of Life.

QUESTIONS: *Fill in the blanks.*

1. Jesus was speaking to a large _____.
   There were _____ men in the crowd.
2. A young boy had a lunch of _____ loaves of
   _____ and _____ fish.
3. Jesus knew the people were hungry in their
   _____.
4. Jesus said that He is the _____ of _____.
5. Jesus satisfies the hunger of our _____.
6. Believing is _____ in _____.
7. _____ _____is a gift from God.
8. God offers eternal life because _____
   _____.

Here are some questions for you to think about and discuss:

1. Are you hungry in your spirit or soul? What can satisfy your hunger?
2. What does "trusting in Jesus" mean?
3. Can you buy eternal life? How can you receive eternal life?
4. How can you grow as a Christian?

VOCABULARY:

1. **disappointed** *(adjective):* not happy; not pleased; not what you expected
2. **souls** *(noun):* the spirits of people; the part of people that never dies

3. **trusting** *(verb):* depending on; having faith even when you do not understand
4. **resurrection** *(noun):* the act of coming back to life after death
5. **deserve** *(verb):* be worthy of; believe that you earn something by your acts or by being good

8 JESUS IS THE LIGHT OF THE WORLD

Memory Verse: ". . . I [Jesus] am the Light of the world. . . ."
     (John 8:12)
Scripture Lesson: John 8:12-20; 12:35-36, 46

Jesus was in city of Jerusalem (juh-REW-suh-lum) for a Jewish holiday. He was at the **Temple**. He was talking to a crowd of people. He was teaching the people about Himself. Jesus said, "I am the Light of the world." In this lesson, we will learn what Jesus meant.

A. JESUS CALLED HIMSELF A LIGHT. (John 8:12, 20)

It was the time of a Jewish holiday. The holiday had a special **ceremony** for lighting candles. There were four large candle holders in the Temple. The candles were lighted after it became dark. The candles burned all night. The light from the candles was very bright. The light took away the darkness of the city.

Jesus told the people, "I am the Light of the world." (verse 12) He meant that He is like the light from the candles. He shines in the **darkness of sin** in the world. The Light is bright. The Light takes away the darkness of sin. And, the Light shines for more than just one night. The Light of Jesus always shines.

Some of the people did not worship the true God. They worshiped the sun. The sun was their god. Jesus told these people that He is the Light of the world. He meant that He is greater and brighter than the sun. He is greater than the sun god or any other false god.

Jesus probably **reminded the people** of their own Scriptures. The writer of the Psalms said, "The Lord is my light . . ." (Psalm 27:1) "Your word is . . . a light for my path." (Psalm 119:105)

Jesus, the Light of the world, can lead us. The Light shows us the way to God. The Light shows us the right way to live.

B. THE PHARISEES (FAIR-uh-seez) DID NOT AGREE WITH JESUS.
     (John 8:13-19)

The Pharisees were Jewish leaders. They taught the Jews about their religion. The Pharisees did not like what Jesus said. They did not believe Jesus. They did not believe that Jesus was the Son of God.

Jesus had told the Pharisees they were in darkness. He told them they were sinners. He said they were wrong. (Read Matthew 23:1-36.) The Pharisees were angry. They were mad because Jesus told them they were wrong.

The law of the Jews said there must be two **witnesses.** Two witnesses were needed to prove something was true. But, Jesus did not have any witnesses. The Pharisees said that Jesus could not prove who He was.

Jesus answered the Pharisees. He said that He did not need a witness. Jesus knew who He was. He knew where He came from and where He was going. Also, Jesus said that God is His witness. God, His Father, sent Jesus to earth. Jesus came to do the work of God. We know God when we know Jesus.

C. JESUS WANTS US TO WALK IN THE LIGHT. (John 12:35-36, 46)

Jesus' work on earth was almost done. He wanted the people to walk in the Light. They needed to walk in the Light before it was too late. Soon, the Light would be gone. Jesus wanted the people to become **sons of the Light.**

Today, Jesus wants us to be sons of the Light. We become sons of the Light by believing in Jesus. We believe that Jesus is the Son of God. We trust Jesus to save us from our sins. Sin is darkness. Sin brings **spiritual death.** Sons of the Light are **delivered** from the darkness of sin and spiritual death.

Sons of the Light walk in the Light. We walk in the Light by following Jesus. We must follow Jesus every day. We must live the way He wants us to live. The Light shows us our sins. The Light shows us if we do something wrong. The Light shows us if we should change something in our lives. We walk in the Light as we obey Jesus. We grow as Christians as we walk in the Light.

Many people are walking in darkness today. They do not know where they are going. They do not know about God. They do know what Jesus taught. They do not walk in the Light. This is darkness. This darkness leads to spiritual death.

If we are walking in darkness, we should turn to the Light. We should turn to the Light while we can. We should turn to Jesus now.

Christians should share the Light of Jesus with other people. All people need to know that the Light can deliver them from the darkness of sin. The Light can show them the way to God.

CONCLUSION

Who is Jesus? Jesus is the Light of the world. The Light shows us the way to God. The Light can deliver us from the darkness of sin. The Light can show how to live. We grow as Christians as we walk in the Light.

QUESTIONS: *Give the answers.*

1. Where was Jesus teaching? _____
2. Who did Jesus tell the people He was? "I am the _____ of the _____."
3. What does the Light take away? _____
4. What does the Light show us? _____
5. Whom do we know when we know Jesus? _____
6. How do we "walk in the Light?" _____
7. How can we grow as Christians? _____
8. What should we share with other people? _____

Here are some questions for you to think about and discuss:

1. How is Jesus the Light of the world?
2. How is the Light of Jesus greater than the light of the sun?
3. How can you "walk in the Light?"
4. Are you sharing the Light of the world with other people? How can you share the Light?

VOCABULARY:

1. **Temple** *(proper noun):* the building for the worship of God in the city of Jerusalem
2. **ceremony** *(noun):* a special act, usually done in the same way each time; A ceremony has special meaning to the people who do it or watch it. The Lord's Supper is a Christian ceremony.
3. **darkness of sin** *(noun phrase):* evil acts or deeds; sins are sometimes called "deeds of darkness;" people are in spiritual darkness because they do not know God.
4. **reminded the people** *(verb phrase):* helped the people to remember; helped the people to think about again

5. **witnesses** *(noun):* people who tell other people what they have seen or know is true; people who see something with their own eyes
6. **sons of the Light** *(noun phrase):* all people who believe in Jesus Christ; people who are saved from sin; children of God
7. **spiritual death** *(noun phrase):* being separated from God; Sinners have spiritual death until they become Christians. Sinners who die go to hell and have spiritual death forever.
8. **delivered** *(verb):* taken out of; be free of; be rid of; no longer a part of

9 | JESUS IS THE GOOD SHEPHERD

Memory Verse: "I [Jesus] am the Good Shepherd . . ." (John 10:14)
Scripture Lesson: John 10:1-15

Sometimes, we may feel that no person cares for us. But, Jesus does. He cares about us very much.

Jesus wanted to let the people know how much He cared for them. So, Jesus called Himself the Good **Shepherd.** He **compared** Himself to a shepherd. And, He compared the people to sheep. Jesus knew that the people knew about shepherds and sheep. He knew they would understand what He was teaching them.

Jesus' words are also for us today. He cares for us as a shepherd cares for his sheep.

A. JESUS KNOWS US BY OUR NAMES. (John 10:1-6)

In Jesus' time, sheep were kept in a **pen.** Several shepherds had their sheep in the same pen. Each shepherd called his sheep by their names. Each shepherd knew his own sheep. And, the sheep knew the voices of their shepherds. The sheep came when their shepherd called them. They followed their shepherd.

Jesus is our Shepherd. We are His sheep. Jesus knows each one of us by our name. He calls us by our names.

When we know Jesus, we know His voice. We know when He is talking to us. Jesus teaches us to listen to His voice. He teaches us not to listen to other voices.

Sheep run away from voices they do not know. We should run away from voices we do not know. These voices will not teach us the truth about God. We must follow only the Good Shepherd. We must listen only to the voice of the Shepherd.

B. JESUS PROTECTS US FROM HARM. (John 10:7-10)

Some sheep pens did not have gates or doors. So, the shepherd became the gate or door for the pen. He would lie down in the door opening. He would protect the sheep from their enemies. The shepherd was the only way to get to the sheep.

The sheep had enemies. Sometimes, wolves tried to kill and eat the sheep. Sometimes, robbers tried to steal sheep out of the pen. But, the shepherd would protect the sheep. The shepherd was the gate to keep the enemies out of the pen.

Jesus is our gate. He is our gate in two ways. First, Jesus is the Way to God. We can only get to God through Jesus. Jesus shows us the way to God. He shows us the way to eternal life. Jesus is the only Way.

Second, Jesus protects us from our enemies. The **devil** and false teachers are our enemies. They try to take us away from God. They tell us that Jesus does not care for us. Their voices do not teach us the truth.

Jesus **warns** us about our enemies. He tells us to be careful. He tells us that our enemies will try to **trick** us. Jesus warns us because He cares for us. He tells us to listen only to His voice. We must not listen to the devil or false teachers.

C. JESUS GAVE HIMSELF FOR US. (John 10:11-15)

The people knew that a good shepherd cared for his sheep. He led his sheep to green **pastures.** He wanted them to have good food. Sometimes, the shepherd carried his sheep. He did not want them to get lost. A good shepherd protected his sheep. He watched his sheep. He looked for any sheep that was lost. He took care of the sheep when they were hurt.

A good shepherd gave his life for his sheep. The people understood this too. Some shepherds were bad shepherds. They did not care for their sheep. They ran away when a wolf or robber came. But, good shepherds did not run away. They stayed to fight the enemy. A few good shepherds even died for their sheep.

Jesus is like the good shepherd. He cares for us. He leads us. He wants us to have what we need. Jesus protects us. He watches over us. Jesus looks for lost sheep. He looks for us when we do not follow Him. He cares for us when we hurt.

Jesus, the Good Shepherd, gave His life for His sheep. Jesus died on the Cross for us. Shepherds sometimes died so their sheep could live. Jesus died so we can live. Jesus cares for us so much that He died so we can have eternal life.

CONCLUSION

Who is Jesus? Jesus is the Good Shepherd. We are His sheep. He knows each one of us and we know Him. We know His voice. We listen to Him.

Jesus cares for us like a shepherd cares for his sheep. He watches over us and protects us. He gave His life for us.

_____

QUESTIONS: *Give the answers.*

1. Whom did Jesus compare Himself to? _____
   _____

2. How does Jesus know us? He knows us by our _____.

3. Whose voice is the only voice we should listen to? _____
   _____

4. What two ways is Jesus our gate?
   (1) _____.
   (2) _____.

5. Who are our enemies? the _____ and false
   _____

6. How did Jesus give His life for us? He _____ on
   the _____.

7. Why did Jesus give His life for us? Because He _____
   us.

8. What kind of people are "lost sheep?" People who do not
   _____.

Here are some questions for you to think about and discuss:

1. How do you know the voice of the Good Shepherd?

2. What do you do when you hear the voices of the devil or false teachers?

3. How is Jesus like a good shepherd?

4. How does Jesus care for you?

_____

VOCABULARY:

1. **shepherd** *(noun):* a person who takes care of sheep

2. **compared** *(verb):* showed how things are alike or the same

3. **pen** *(noun):* a small place outside where animals, mostly sheep, are kept

4. **devil** *(noun):* Satan; the most powerful of evil spirits; the enemy of God
5. **warns** *(verb):* tells someone of danger or harm that may happen
6. **trick** *(verb):* make someone think a thing is true when it is not true; Usually a person does not tell the truth when he tricks someone else.
7. **pastures** *(noun):* fields of grass where animals eat

10 JESUS IS THE RESURRECTION AND THE LIFE

Memory Verse: ". . . I [Jesus] am the Resurrection and the Life. . . ."
  (John 11:25)
Scripture Lesson: John 11:17-27, 38-44
Background Lesson: John 11:1-16

Mary and Martha (MAHR-thuh) were sisters. They had a brother named Lazarus (LAZ-uh-rus). They lived in the town of Bethany (BETH-uh-nee). Mary, Martha, and Lazarus were very good friends of Jesus. He often stayed with them in their home.

One day, Lazarus became sick. His sisters knew that Jesus could help him. But, Jesus was not there. They sent a message to Jesus. They told Him that Lazarus was sick. But, Lazarus died before Jesus got to Bethany. Mary and Martha buried their brother.

A. ALL **HOPE** FOR LIFE WAS GONE. (John 11:17-20)

Jesus was on His way to Bethany with His disciples. Martha heard that Jesus was coming. She ran to meet Him, but Mary stayed at home. Many friends were there too. They were **mourning** the death of Lazarus. He had been buried for four days.

Many Jews hoped a dead person would come back to life. So, they believed that the soul or spirit stayed near the body after death. They believed the soul would stay nearby for three days. Then, the soul would leave. Then, the person was dead. Then, all hope for life was gone.

Lazarus had been buried for four days. His soul was gone. His family and friends were sad. They had lost all hope for him. They were mourning. Lazarus was dead. Nothing could change this fact.

B. JESUS GAVE HOPE FOR LIFE. (John 11:21-27)

Martha met Jesus on the road. She told Jesus that He could have helped Lazarus. If Jesus had been there, her brother would not have died. Martha believed in the power of Jesus. But, now her hope was gone too. Lazarus was dead.

Jesus said that Lazarus would live again. Martha said she knew her brother would live in the resurrection. Martha believed in the resurrection at the last day. (verse 24) She believed that Christians will live again in the future. But, she did not believe Lazarus would come back to life right then.

Jesus said that He is the Resurrection and the Life. (verse 25) He does not just give life. Jesus is Life. Jesus is **Resurrection Life.**

Jesus said that physical death is not the final death. The final death is **eternal death.** Eternal death is for people who do not believe in Jesus. But, there is hope! Final death does not have to come after physical death. Resurrection life can come after physical death. Resurrection life is eternal life. Jesus gives eternal life to everyone who believes in Him.

Jesus asked Martha if she believed in Him. Martha said "yes." She believed that Jesus is the Christ, the Son of God. (verse 27) Martha believed. But, her hope was only a hope for the future.

C. JESUS SHOWED HIS POWER OVER DEATH. (John 11:38-44)

Jesus went to the tomb where Lazarus was buried. There was a large stone over the door of the tomb. Jesus said to take away the stone. But Martha **protested.** She said that her brother had been buried for four days. The **odor** would be very bad. The smell of death would be great.

Jesus told Martha that she would see the glory of God. So, the stone was taken away from the door. Jesus prayed to God. He prayed so the people would believe in Him. Many people were there. They were mourning with Mary and Martha. Jesus wanted them to believe that He was the Son of God. He wanted them to see the glory of God. Jesus wanted them to have hope. He wanted them to have the hope of eternal life.

Then, Jesus called Lazarus out of the tomb. Lazarus, the dead man, came out of the tomb. His hands and feet were wrapped with linen cloth. His face was wrapped with a burial cloth. Jesus told the people to take off the cloths. He said to let Lazarus go. Lazarus was alive! This was a great miracle!

CONCLUSION

Who is Jesus? He is the Resurrection and the Life.

Lazarus was raised from the dead. Mary, Martha, and the other people saw the glory of God. The glory of God was His power over death. The glory of God was His power to give life.

Today, we can see the glory of God. We can see the power and glory of God when we believe. We have hope when we believe in Jesus. We have hope for eternal life. We do not need to fear physical death. Jesus gives us life. He is the Resurrection and the Life.

QUESTIONS: *Give the answers.*

1. Who were the three friends of Jesus? _____,
   _____, and _____

2. Where did Jesus' friends live? _____

3. What happened to Lazarus? _____

4. Who believed that Jesus could help Lazarus? _____

5. Who did Jesus say that He was? "I am the
   _____ and the _____."

6. What is the final death?
   _____ _____

7. Why did Jesus pray at Lazarus' tomb? _____
   _____

8. How can we have hope? When _____
   _____.

Here are some questions for you to think about and discuss:

1. Why did Jesus say, "I am the Resurrection and the Life?"
2. Do you see the glory of God today? In what things do you see God's glory?
3. How is Jesus our Hope?
4. How can we have hope in an evil world? What happens when we have hope?

VOCABULARY:

1. **hope** *(noun):* the belief that life will be better in the future; the belief in eternal life; the belief that God will do what He has promised; trusting God for a better future
2. **mourning** *(verb):* being sad over a person's death; having great sorrow; showing grief
3. **Resurrection Life** *(noun phrase):* eternal life; life after death

4. **eternal death** *(noun phrase):* being separated from God forever; being punished in hell forever

5. **protested** *(verb):* said that you did not agree with something; complained

6. **odor** *(noun):* a strong smell; something that causes the sense of smell to act

11 JESUS IS THE GIVER OF THE HOLY SPIRIT

Memory Verse: ". . . you will receive the gift of the Holy Spirit."
   (Acts 2:38)
Scripture Lesson: John 14:15-27
Background Lesson: John 13:33—14:14

The disciples of Jesus left everything to follow Him. They left their jobs, homes, and families. The disciples loved Jesus more than those things. They believed that He was the Messiah.

Later, Jesus told the disciples that He was leaving them. At first, they did not believe what Jesus said. Then, they asked Jesus where He was going. They asked why they could not go with Him. The disciples were afraid. They were worried. They were disappointed.

Jesus talked to His disciples. He **encouraged** them with His words. Today, the words of Jesus are for us too. His words encourage and help us.

A. JESUS TAUGHT ABOUT TRUE LOVE. (John 14:15, 21-24)

Jesus said, "If you love Me, you will obey what I command." (verse 15) This means we will obey Him. We will do everything He tells us to do.

Our love for Jesus is more than a feeling of love. It is more than knowing what Jesus wants us to do. These are good, but they are not enough. We show Jesus that we love Him when we obey Him. When we obey Jesus, we really love Him. But, when we disobey Jesus, we do not love Jesus.

We need to show Jesus that we are thankful for His love. We show we are thankful by our lives. We live to please Jesus in all we do. We love other people as we love ourselves. This is true love.

B. JESUS PROMISED THE HOLY SPIRIT. (John 14:16-17, 25-26)

Jesus said He would ask the Father for the Holy Spirit. He would give the Holy Spirit to the disciples. The Holy Spirit would be with them. He would be with them after Jesus left the earth.

Jesus called the Holy Spirit a **Counselor.** He also called the Holy Spirit the Spirit of Truth. The Holy Spirit would be with them forever.

Jesus said the **world** will not know the Holy Spirit. Only Christians will know the Holy Spirit. They will know the Holy Spirit because He will live in them. They will know Him because He will be with them always.

Today, we need the Holy Spirit. He is our Counselor or Helper. He helps us to live as Christians. We cannot live as Christians by ourselves. The Holy Spirit helps us live to please Jesus.

The Holy Spirit helps us to know the truth. He is the Spirit of Truth. He teaches us about God. He helps us to understand the Word of God. He reminds us of all that Jesus taught.

C. JESUS IS ALWAYS WITH US. (John 14:18-20)

Jesus said that He would not leave the disciples as **orphans.** He promised to be with them. And He kept His promise. He gave them the Holy Spirit. Jesus was with them in the Holy Spirit. They were not alone.

For a while, the disciples had Jesus **in person** with them. Today, we do not have Jesus in person. But, we do have Him with us in Spirit. He lives in us through the Holy Spirit. Jesus gives us His Spirit to be in us. What a wonderful gift!

D. JESUS PROMISED PEACE. (John 14:27)

Jesus was going to leave His disciples soon. The disciples were sad. They were afraid. They were worried about living with Jesus gone. So, Jesus promised them peace. He told them not to be worried or afraid.

Today, Jesus also promises us peace. This does not mean there will be no war. This does not mean we will not have problems. We live on this earth. There will always be war on the earth. There will always be many problems. But, we can have Jesus' peace inside of us.

Our peace comes from our **salvation.** Jesus has **control** of our lives when we are saved. We can have peace because Jesus is in control. Jesus has control of the world. He can take care of us. He will help us with our problems. He will lead and guide us. Jesus is with us through the Holy Spirit. And where Jesus is, there is peace.

CONCLUSION

Who is Jesus? He is the Giver of the Holy Spirit. Today, we do not have Jesus with us in person. But, we have the Holy Spirit. Jesus is with us through the Holy Spirit. He helps us live as Christians. He helps us know the truth. He gives us peace. He is always with us. Let us thank God for the gift of the Holy Spirit.

QUESTIONS: *Fill in the blanks.*

1. We show Jesus that we love Him when we _____
   Him.
2. Jesus promised to give the _____
   _____ to the disciples.
3. Jesus called the Holy Spirit a _____.
   He also called Him the _____ of
   _____.
4. The Holy Spirit helps us to live as _____
5. The Holy Spirit helps us to understand the _____
   of _____.
6. Today, _____ is with us through the Holy Spirit.
7. The Holy Spirit gives us_____ inside of us. This
   peace comes from our _____.
8. Jesus, through the Holy Spirit, will help us with our
   _____.

Here are some questions for you to think about and discuss:

1. Do you love Jesus? How can you show Him that you love Him?
2. How is the Holy Spirit your Helper?
3. How is the Holy Spirit your Teacher?
4. Do you have the peace Jesus gives? How do you know He is in
   control of the world?

VOCABULARY:

1. **encouraged** *(verb):* said words to help a person feel better; gave
   hope to
2. **counselor** *(noun):* someone who listens to you and helps you
   with your problems; the Holy Spirit
3. **world** *(noun):* the people on earth who do not believe in Jesus as
   their Savior; people who are not Christians
4. **orphans** *(noun):* people, usually children, whose parents have
   died

5. **in person** *(prepositional phrase):* being present in body so that people can see and know a person is alive
6. **salvation** *(noun):* the act of God by which He saves people from sin and hell
7. **control** *(noun):* the act of ruling; having power over; in charge of

12 JESUS IS THE VINE

Memory Verse: "I am the Vine; you are the branches. . . ." (John 15:5)
Scripture Lesson: John 15:1-17

We have been studying who Jesus is. In this lesson, Jesus said that He is the Vine. This does not mean Jesus is a vine. This means that Jesus compared Himself to a grape vine. He also compared His disciples to branches of the vine. And, He compared God, the Father, to a gardener. Jesus used a grape vine to teach His disciples. He used the vine to talk about the **relationship** between Himself and His followers. This lesson is an important lesson for us today.

A. THE VINE MUST BE **PRUNED.** (John 15:1-4)

A gardener prunes grape vines as a part of his job. He prunes the vines to help them grow and **produce** grapes. A vine produces more fruit when it is pruned. It also produces better fruit when it is pruned.

A gardener cuts off the branches that are dead. Dead branches cannot produce grapes. Sometimes, the gardener cuts off some of the living branches. But, he only prunes certain branches. These branches are still living. But, they are not producing fruit.

Today, God prunes the Vine. This means that He cuts off the dead branches. And, He prunes all the branches that do not produce fruit. These branches are the Christians who no longer live for Jesus. They are no longer living in Jesus, the Vine. They are not producing fruit in their Christian lives. They stop loving Jesus. They do not obey Jesus. They do not tell other people about Him.

The good branches are the people who follow Jesus Christ. They are living in Him. They produce "fruit." They love and obey Jesus. They serve Jesus. They witness for Him.

B. THE VINE'S BRANCHES MUST PRODUCE FRUIT. (John 15:5-8)

Branches on the Vine will produce much fruit. (verse 5) This means Christians will produce fruit in their lives. What "fruit" can Christians produce?

One type of fruit is witnessing. We must tell other people about Jesus. But, witnessing is only one part of the Christian life.

We must live in Jesus. We only produce "fruit" when we live in Jesus. Living in Jesus is living a Christian life. It is having a right relationship with Jesus. We live in Jesus as we pray and study the Bible. We live in Jesus as we obey and serve Him. This is how we produce fruit. But, we cannot produce fruit by ourselves. Jesus said we can do nothing unless we live in Him. (verse 5)

Jesus gave a **warning**. The warning is for the people who stop living in Jesus. They will be cut off from the Vine. They will be thrown away. They will die because they are no longer a part of the Vine.

Jesus also gave a promise. The promise is for the people who live in the Vine. The promise is for **faithful** Christians. Their prayers will be answered. Then, God will receive the glory. God is praised when Christians produce fruit in their lives.

C. THE VINE COMMANDED THE BRANCHES TO LOVE.
(John 15:9-17)

Jesus said that His Father loved Him. In the same way, Jesus loves us. (verse 9) From their **examples**, we learn to love. We love because we are loved. We love Jesus because He loves us.

We must obey Jesus to stay in His love. (verse 10) We must do what He tells us to do. We must obey Jesus to have the right relationship with Him. Then, we are living in Jesus, the Vine.

Jesus commanded us to "love each other." (verses 12 and 17) The greatest love we can have is to give our lives for our friends. Jesus had this type of love. Jesus gave His life for us. He died on the Cross for our sins. This is the type of love we should have.

We give our lives by loving Jesus. We give our lives by living in Jesus. And, we give our lives by loving other people.

Our love must **go beyond** our friends and families. We must love all people in the world. We must love all people in the way Jesus loves us.

Our relationship with Jesus is important. And, we have the right relationship with Jesus by obeying Him. Then, we are "good branches" living in "the Vine."

CONCLUSION

Who is Jesus? He is the Vine. He gives us life. We grow as we live in Him. But, we must love and obey Him. We must love other people as He loves us. Then, we are "branches" that produce much "fruit" in our lives.

QUESTIONS: *Fill in the blanks.*

1. _____ is the Vine and we are the
   _____.

2. God _____ all the branches that do not produce
   _____.

3. Good branches are people who _____ Jesus. They
   _____ and _____ Him.

4. One type of "fruit" is _____.

5. Jesus commands us to _____.

6. _____ gave His life for us. He _____
   _____ for our sins.

7. We give our lives by _____ _____
   and by loving _____ _____.

8. We have the right _____ with
   Jesus by _____ Him.

Here are some questions for you to think about and discuss:

1. How can you live in Jesus, the Vine?

2. Are you a "living branch" that is producing fruit? How can you
   produce "fruit" in your life?

3. How did Jesus show His love for you?

4. How can you love other people?

5. How can you have the right relationship with Jesus?

VOCABULARY:

1. **relationship** *(noun):* the act of being joined together for certain
   reasons; The relationship between Jesus and people is based on
   people believing Jesus is God's Son. We believe that Jesus is the
   Savior and that He saves us from sin.

2. **pruned** *(verb):* cut branches off a plant or tree

3. **produce** *(verb):* make; grow; have

4. **warning** *(noun):* letting people know about something before it happens; Warning usually means that something bad is going to happen.
5. **faithful** *(adjective):* loyal and true
6. **examples** *(noun):* people we should try to be like; models for other people; Christians should try to be like God and His Son, Jesus.
7. **go beyond** (verb phrase): be more than; be greater than

13 JESUS IS OUR INTERCESSOR

Memory Verse: ". . . Christ Jesus . . . is at the right hand of God and is also **interceding** for us." (Romans 8:34)
Scripture Lesson: John 17:9-23

Jesus had been with His disciples for about three years. He had taught them many things. Then, He told them He was going to leave them. But, He promised to send the Holy Spirit to help them.

It was the night before Jesus was crucified. He was eating a meal with His disciples. He talked with them a long time. Then, Jesus prayed. He prayed for the disciples. He also prayed for all people who believed in Him. He interceded to God for His followers. Jesus' prayer is for us too.

A. FOLLOWERS OF JESUS BELONG TO GOD. (John 17:9-12)

Jesus prayed for His disciples. He prayed that they would remain true followers.

Jesus did not pray for the world. (verse 9) Jesus loved the world. He wanted all people to be saved. But, the world will only be saved when Christians **fulfill their mission.** The world will be saved when Christians witness and tell others about Jesus. So, Jesus prayed for His followers.

When we are saved, we become God's **property.** Christians belong to God. We are His children. But, we still live on this earth. And, this earth is evil. So, Jesus prayed that God would protect His children. (verse 11)

Jesus also prayed that His followers would be one. (verse 11) The Father and Jesus are One. They are One because they are God. They agree on their purposes. They agree that people should be saved. Christians are one because they belong to God. Christians are one when they have the same mission.

B. FOLLOWERS OF JESUS ARE **PROTECTED**. (John 17:13-16)

Jesus was *in* the world, but He was not *of* the world. This means that Jesus lived on earth. He lived as a person like all other people live in the world. But, Jesus did not sin. He did not do evil things. He did not live like the sinful people. He obeyed God in all things. He was not *of* the world.

Christians are like Jesus. They are *in* the world, but they are not *of* the world. Christians live on earth, but they do not do evil things. They do not live like sinful people. They obey God.

Jesus interceded to God for His followers. Jesus prayed that they would be safe. Jesus did not ask God to take His followers out of the world. He asked God to protect them in the world. He prayed that God would protect His followers from Satan and evil. (verse 15)

C. FOLLOWERS OF JESUS ARE **SANCTIFIED.** (John 17:17-19)

Jesus asked God to sanctify His followers. In this scripture, sanctify means to set apart for a holy mission. It means to be sanctified to do the work of God. It means to be called out of the world to belong to God completely.

God, the Father, sent Jesus into the world. Jesus was set apart by God for a special mission. Jesus told other people about God. He showed people who God is. He died for the sins of all people.

Jesus gave the disciples a holy mission. He sent them into the world. (verse 18) He told them to be His witnesses. Jesus interceded to God for the disciples. He prayed that they would be sanctified. He prayed that God would set them apart to be witnesses of the gospel.

D. FOLLOWERS OF JESUS ARE **UNITED.** (John 17:20-23)

Jesus prayed for more than the 12 disciples. He interceded to God for all people who believe the gospel. And His prayer is for all Christians today.

Jesus prayed that all Christians would be united. Jesus prayed that we might become one. We become one in God. When we are united, we love each other. When we are united, we pray for each other. When we are united, we work together. The world will see that we are one. Then, the world will believe in Jesus Christ. Then, the world will know that God loves them. (verse 23) The best way for Christians to witness is for Christians to be united.

CONCLUSION

Who is Jesus? He is our **Intercessor.** Jesus interceded to God for His followers. He prayed that they would remain true followers. He prayed for their protection from evil in the world. He prayed that they would be sanctified to do the work of God. He prayed that they would be united. When this happens, the world will believe in the gospel of Jesus.

Today, Jesus is our Intercessor. He is with God, the Father, in heaven. He intercedes for us to God. When we pray, Jesus hears us. He asks God to answers our prayers. We can trust Jesus because He loves us.

QUESTIONS: *Give the answers.*

1. Whom did Jesus pray for? _____

2. How will the world be saved? When Christians _____

   _____

3. Whom do followers of Jesus belong to? _____

4. From what did Jesus pray that God would protect us? From

   _____ and _____

5. Why are Jesus' followers sanctified or set apart? _____

   _____

6. What is the best way for Christians to witness? _____

   _____

7. Where is Jesus today? Look at the memory verse.

   _____

8. What is Jesus doing today for us? _____

Here are some questions for you to think about and discuss:

1. Do you belong to God? How do you know you are God's child?

2. Are you *in* the world or *of* the world? How can you be *in* the world but not *of* the world?

3. How has Jesus protected you?

4. Are you fulfilling your holy mission? How are you witnessing for Jesus Christ?

5. Jesus is our Intercessor. Can Christians intercede to God for other people? Why (or why not) do you think so?

VOCABULARY:

1. **interceding** *(verb):* praying for another person or other people
2. **fulfill their mission** *(verb phrase):* do what they have been told to do; witness to people; share with people the gospel message
3. **property** *(noun):* things that are owned; things that belong to a person
4. **protected** *(verb):* taken care of; made safe; kept from harm and danger
5. **sanctified** *(verb):* set apart for a holy purpose; made holy
6. **united** *(adjective):* together in purpose; made as one
7. **Intercessor** *(noun):* a person who prays for another person or for other people; In this lesson, the Intercessor is Jesus.

Introduction for Teachers

The intercultural English lessons in this book have been developed for people who are developing proficiency in English. The intended audience includes bilingual speakers, such as new immigrants and ESL (English as a second language) learners, and English speakers who are preliterate and learning disabled. Also, new Christians and people with a limited knowledge of Bible truths can benefit by the simple, brief lessons. Such people can profit from materials with a controlled vocabulary and sentence structure to help them better understand the Bible and Christian concepts.

The target audience is the intermediate-level student who can work comfortably with a 2,200-word vocabulary. The writers, therefore, have been given careful consideration to both the vocabulary and sentence structure.

New words and phrases, ten items or less, have been introduced in each lesson. The words/phrases appear in the vocabulary list as they appear in the lesson text, both in form and sequence. The parts of speech have been included as an aid for teaching English.

In applying linguistic controls, the language has been simplified. The writers have purposely sacrificed style for simplicity in order to obtain English at a level that is more easily read and understood by the target audience.

The lessons, based on previously-written Bible studies, have been adapted to **Intercultural English** to serve as transition materials while the learners are gaining Bible knowledge and English skills. The adaptation has also involved deleting content and language (such as illustrations, examples, poetry, figures of speech, etc.) that may be inappropriate in a cross-cultural learning situation.

There are two appendixes in this section, *Teacher Resources.* Appendix A contains suggested answers to the study questions. Appendix B includes several useful tips for teaching. Teachers should become familiar with this supplementary information.

We believe this type of Bible study material meets a vital need that exists today in evangelical Christianity. We pray that God will honor His Word as it becomes a part of the learners' minds—**and hearts**—through the medium of **Intercultural English.**

J. Wesley Eby

APPENDIX A

ANSWERS TO QUESTIONS

For each lesson there is a set of suggested answers for the study questions. You will find the intended answers, along with some possible alternatives or extensions (in parentheses), which are all correct in the context of the lessons. Teachers should be willing to accept any answer that can be justified.

Lesson 1
1. Son of God
2. belief and trust in God
3. eternal life
4. world (all things; life)
5. the Word
6. God
7. children of God
8. (1) Jesus is our Savior. (He gives us eternal life.)
   (2) God created everything through Jesus, His Son.
   (3) Jesus shows us who God is and what God is like.

Lesson 2
1. Christ (Messiah)
2. Messiah; prophets
3. greater
4. faith
5. Savior; sin
6. Holy Spirit
7. witnesses
8. Jesus Christ

Lesson 3
1. (to the city of) Jerusalem
2. (their) king
3. Palm Sunday
4. prophecies
5. to give life to us (to save us from our sins)
6. our lives

7. God (Jesus)
8. eternal life (our glory)

Lesson 4
1. Jesus (Christ)
2. He died on a cross.
3. Mary (Magdalene) (also, Peter and John)
4. That robbers had taken (stolen) Jesus' body.
5. When Jesus said Mary's name.
6. personal relationship
7. (the) Holy Spirit
8. Jesus is alive! (He is our living Lord!)

Lesson 5
1. eternal life
2. God
3. anyone (everyone; all people)
4. sins
5. way
6. forgives; repent
7. God; Jesus
8. Way; Life

Lesson 6
1. Jews (Israelites); Samaritans
2. He [Jesus] asked her for a drink of water. (He talked to her.)

3. God loves us.
4. living water
5. eternal life: new life in Jesus
6. Messiah
7. She told all the people.
8. (our) spiritual thirst

Lesson 7
1. crowd; 5,000
2. five (5); bread; two (2)
3. spirits (souls)
4. Bread; Life
5. souls (spirits)
6. trusting; Jesus (His death and resurrection)
7. Eternal life
8. He [God] loves us.

Lesson 8
1. (the city of) Jerusalem (at the Temple)
2. Light; world
3. (darkness of) sin
4. the way to God (the right way to live)
5. God (the Father)
6. by following Jesus (as we obey Jesus)
7. walk in the Light
8. (the Light of) Jesus

Lesson 9
1. (a) good shepherd
2. names
3. (the Good) Shepherd (Jesus)
4. (1) He is the Way to God. (2) He protects us from our enemies.
5. devil; teachers
6. died; Cross
7. cares for (loves)
8. follow Him (Jesus)

Lesson 10
1. Mary; Martha; Lazarus
2. (in the town of) Bethany

3. He died. (He became sick and died.)
4. Martha
5. Resurrection; Life
6. eternal death
7. so the people would believe in Him [Jesus]
8. we believe in Jesus

Lesson 11
1. obey
2. Holy Spirit
3. Counselor; Spirit; Truth
4. Christians
5. Word; God
6. Jesus
7. peace; salvation
8. problems

Lesson 12
1. Jesus; branches
2. prunes; fruit
3. follow; love; obey
4. witnessing
5. love one another (love other people)
6. Jesus; died (on the Cross)
7. loving Jesus; other people
8. relationship; obeying

Lesson 13
1. His followers (His disciples; all people who believed Him)
2. fulfill their mission (witness and tell others about Jesus)
3. God
4. Satan; evil
5. to be witnesses of the gospel (for a holy mission; to do the work of God)
6. to be united (to be one)
7. at the right hand of God (in heaven)
8. interceding (praying to God)

APPENDIX B
TEACHING HELPS

A. **Plan carefully and prayerfully.** Anything important enough to do is important enough to plan to do. Unplanned teaching usually results in disorganized instruction, resulting in minimal learning. A familiar maxim says, "If I fail to plan, I plan to fail." Your students are worthy of your careful planning and sincere prayers. Commit your teaching and the learners to God. He will help you as you do your best.

B. **Be sensitive to the learners' needs.** Your students will probably be at different levels, both in their Bible knowledge and language skills. Your task, which is not an easy one, is to discover *where* the learners are in their English skills and in their understanding of the Christian faith.

Be aware, also, that the learners' *felt needs* may be different from their *real needs.* But their *felt needs* usually must be met first before you are able to help them with their *real needs.* In your class, you may find the *felt need* is to learn to read while the *real need* is to learn about God. And while you strive to meet the perceived or *felt need,* never lose sight of the *real need.*

There is no special method to help you make this discovery. You DO need to become a people-watcher, however. Look for any hints the students may give in their body language and in what they say. Also, become involved in the learners' lives, both in and out of class. This will help you become much more aware of their backgrounds, their culture, their experiences, and, thus, their needs, *felt and real.* God will be faithful as you commit this *discovery process* to Him.

C. **Determine your objective.** An objective is the purpose for teaching. Your objective or aim, as a Christian teacher, is twofold: Bible content and English language skills. Knowing *what* you are teaching, and *why,* will help you be more confident as a teacher or tutor. As a result, your instruction will be more effective. Therefore, become familiar with the lesson content and, if possible, the language skills needed by the learners.

D. **Focus on comprehension.** This is extremely important! If the learners do not understand, your instruction will be of limited value. Of course, every student will not fully understand everything you teach. But, as a teacher or tutor, try to have each student take away some learning from each session. How much the students understand and learn will vary from person to person. Yet, as a teacher or tutor, your task is to faithfully plant the seeds of God's Word. Then the Holy Spirit will help those seeds to grow and bear fruit in the minds and hearts of the learners.

Some strategies for aiding comprehension are:

1. *Use easy-to-understand Bibles,* such as:
   - *The Everyday Bible (New Century Version).* Thomas Nelson, Inc., P.O. Box 141000, Nashville, TN 33214-1000. <www.nelsonbibles.com>
   - *Contemporary English Version.* 1995. American Bible Society, 1865 Broadway, New York, NY 10023. <www.bibles.com>
   - *Good News Bible: Today's English Version.* 1976. American Bible Society, 1865 Broadway, New York, NY 10023. <www.bibles.com>
   - *Holy Bible: New Life Version.* 1969. Christian Literature International, P.O. Box 777, Canby, OR 97013. <www.newlifebible.org>

   If the students are not native speakers of English, have the students read the Scripture in their first language. This will certainly aid their understanding. Some sources of Bibles in various languages are:
   - The American Bible Society, 1865 Broadway, New York, NY 10023. <www.bibles.com>
   - International Bible Society, 1820 Jet Stream Dr., Colorado Springs, CO 80921. <www.ibs.org>
   - Multi-Language Media, P.O. Box 301, Ephrata, PA 17522. <www.multilanguage.com>

2. *Use the students' first language also, if their native language is other than English.* This is ideal and will result in the greatest amount of learning. If an interpreter is available, or if you know the language, use both languages in your teaching. If possible, give the interpreter the material to be taught before the class session so he/she can become familiar with the lesson content.

3. *Take additional time to teach a lesson, as needed.* You can divide a lesson into two or more parts, according to the needs of the learners. *Remember:* You're teaching people, not materials. Materials are only tools by which you accomplish your objectives or aims.

4. *Tell the learners what you plan to teach as you begin a lesson.* Make the students aware of the lesson content at the beginning of the class. Then after you have taught, give a brief review. Thus, the lesson plan should include these three steps: (1) telling what you are going to teach, (2) teaching, and (3) telling what you have just taught.

5. *Use the questions in the lessons as a part of your teaching.* Questions are an important part of teaching. If time permits, use the questions as a part of the lessons. Or if time is limited, assign the questions for home study and discuss them during the next class session as review and reinforcement. Avoid grading the answers in such a way that the students have a sense of failure. (See Section E.) *Note:* If the questions are an out-of-class assignment, be aware that other family members or friends may help answer the questions.

6. *Don't assume the learners can read the lessons on their own.* If the learners cannot read English, teach the lessons orally. Once the students seem to be reading independently, don't assume they understand what they are reading. Pronouncing the words does not necessarily mean they can read with comprehension. Use oral questions and discussion to help you determine how much they understand.

7. *Work with new and unknown words both before and during the lesson.* Develop vocabulary in meaningful activities, avoiding word lists. Many of the high-frequency words of English (such as *the, but, or, of, by, because*) have limited or no meaning by themselves. Also, many nouns and verbs have multiple meanings. Vocabulary has little value if there is no useful meanings for the learners. Always work with words in phrases or sentences that have meaning for your students. Make flash cards by writing the new word on the front, and write sentences with the word on the back. Also, be careful in the use of idioms, figures of speech, and slang expressions.

8. *Add your own examples and stories that are appropriate for the lessons.* Nonbiblical examples and stories are not included since such examples and stories are different from culture to culture. Yet, such stories or examples are very effective in the learning process, Just make certain the stories, examples, or illustrations are appropriate and meaningful for your learners.

9. *Use real objects, pictures, and other audiovisual aids, as much as possible.* Bulletin boards, charts, flash cards, cassette tapes, etc., will make the lessons more effective.

Teach for success. This begins, of course, with focusing on comprehension. If the learners understand, then you should expect success.

1. *Give sincere praise.* Help the students know they are learning. Reinforce their self-worth as individuals and as God's children, created in His image.

2. *Capitalize on the learners' strengths and their correct responses.* Minimize their weaknesses and mistakes.

3. *Assume every student WANTS to learn, CAN learn, and WILL learn.* Then teach according to this belief.

Be a good language model. This is essential since people are introduced to language by listening to it. This is true for all native and most non-native English speakers. As a language model, however, you do not have to be perfect. Discard any worries you may have. Just be yourself, and do the best you can. Try these practical ideas:

1. *Be natural.* Use spoken English as it is naturally used by native English speakers. Be careful not to talk down to the learners by using "baby talk."

2. *Talk slowly.* Most learners, especially second language learners, better understand language if spoken a little slower than used in normal speech. Yet, the speaker must maintain appropriate volume, rhythm, stress, and phrasing. Some teachers err by increasing volume as they slow down their speech. The increased volume is often misinterpreted by the learners.

3. *Be clear in pronunciation.* Pronounce words distinctly, making certain that you do not omit or slur final consonant sounds. Try to be clear and precise in your pronunciation while retaining naturalness.

   Don't expect adults or older youth who are learning English as a second language to speak it as native speakers. Research indicates that the learners will probably always speak it with an accent. *Remember:* The goal is for the learners to be able to communicate in English. They can accomplish this goal even if their pronunciation is not perfect.

4. *Model correct language.* This is an important technique, especially for correcting mistakes. You can show the correct response, language usage, or pronunciation simply by "doing it" yourself. Don't require the students to correct all their mistakes. For each lesson, focus on only one or two mistakes you would like the learners to correct and master. Pointing out too many errors at a time can be discouraging and embarrassing for the learners.

5. *Read aloud often.* You, as the teacher or tutor, can model good reading and oral language as you read aloud to the students. Research indicates this is a valuable technique. And as you read, be expressive and enthusiastic.

   Students need to hear you read the Scriptures frequently as well as the entire lesson. Read a Bible passage or the lesson aloud first before the learners ever see it. Then, read it a second time while they follow along with their eyes. This provides them with needed auditory (ear) and visual (eye) introduction to the lesson before they read it on their own.

EDITOR'S NOTE:

This information on teaching is extremely limited. Entire textbooks have been written on this subject. Space requirements, however, require that this supplementary material be brief. I pray, though, that what you have read will assist you as you minister to your students.

J. Wesley Eby